Naples & Amalfi Coast Travel Guide

The Ultimate Pocket Guide to Simplify Your Trip-Planning Process | Explore Naples' Archaeological Museum, Pompeii Forum and Indulge in Authentic Pizza

Ciro Di Giovanni

Table of Contents

Introduction

Have you ever felt the pull of wanderlust, where your spirit yearns for stunning scenery and your heart yearns for fresh experiences? Imagine yourself ambling down cobblestone streets while the aroma of hot, freshly made pizza fills the air and the brilliant turquoise waters glitter in the rays of the Mediterranean sun. We cordially invite you to explore the enchanted world of Napples and the Amalfi Coast, where fantasies come true and reality and fantasy meld together beautifully.

With the help of this fascinating travel book, we cordially encourage you to set off on a discovery-filled tour to two amazing locales that have won the hearts of millions: Napples, the alluring city of paradoxes, and the Amalfi Coast, Italy's ageless jewel. But let's first take a quick look at these places' significance and history before we discover their riches.

A vivid history that extends back to the time of the ancient Greeks is held by Napples, a city that is located in the Gulf of Naples. Napples has developed from its modest beginnings as a bustling fishing community into a thriving metropolis, overflowing with life, culture, and a zest for la dolce vita. This city has influenced innumerable artists, writers, and visionaries throughout history thanks to its rich legacy.

On the other side, the Amalfi Coast has mesmerized tourists with its unparalleled natural beauty for decades. You'll come across lovely settlements built on precipitous cliffs that provide breath-taking vistas of the Tyrrhenian Sea as you meander down the picturesque coastal roads. The Amalfi Coast, which was once a maritime superpower, still exudes echoes of its illustrious past in the form of picturesque fishing villages and medieval buildings.

We comprehend your need to escape the everyday, find consolation in new horizons, and lose yourself in the allure of these remarkable places. The difficulties of organizing a trip, navigating uncharted territory, and finding hidden gems can frequently be insurmountable. We created this complete guide to solve your issues and pains in order to make your experience easy and memorable.

Your Napples and Amalfi Coast vacation will become a once-in-a-lifetime experience if you delve into the pages of this book and discover a wealth of priceless knowledge, insider secrets, and insider recommendations. This guide is your key to unlocking the treasures that await you, with thorough itineraries, suggestions on lodging, food, and transportation, fascinating historical insights, and lesser-known locations.

I, the author of this guide and your dependable travel companion, am a knowledgeable and enthusiastic traveler of these captivating locales. Years of first-hand knowledge have allowed me to unearth the hidden jewels, adopt the culture, and build relationships with the vivacious locals that give Napples and the Amalfi Coast life. Every page exudes the author's knowledge of and passion for these locations, giving you the assurance that this is the book for you.

Prepare to set out on a transforming journey across the alluring lands of Napples and the Amalfi Coast, my fellow traveler. As you immerse yourself in the enchantment that lies ahead, let the tastes, smells, and echoes of history guide you. You'll experience the magnetic pull of adventure the moment you open this book, kindling your imagination and luring you into a setting that has the potential to leave a lasting impression on your soul.

Chapter 1: Travel Essentials

Best time to visit.

The best time to visit Naples and the Amalfi Coast depends on your preferences and what activities you want to engage in. Here's a breakdown of the seasons and the corresponding tourist activities to help you make an informed decision:

1. Spring (March to May): Naples and the Amalfi Coast are frequently visited throughout the spring. Temperatures often range from 15°C to 20°C (59°F to 68°F) due to the temperate climate. Without the oppressive summer heat, it's a perfect time to explore the region's cultural sites, such Pompeii and Herculaneum. You can also take in the stunning blossoms and vibrant scenery along the coast.
2. Summer (June to August): Naples and the Amalfi Coast see their busiest travel period in the summer. Weather conditions are hot and sunny, with average

highs of 30 °C (86 °F). The greatest time to take advantage of the breathtaking beaches, the clean waters, water sports, and boat cruises is now. But around this season, expect bigger crowds and more expensive items.

3. Autumn (September to November): Another great time to travel to the area is in the fall. Temperatures range from 18°C to 25°C (64°F to 77°F), and the weather is still pleasant. It's less crowded than the summer, which makes it the perfect time to visit the quaint coastal villages like Positano, Amalfi, and Ravello. The local vineyards' grape harvest can also be observed in the autumn.

4. Winter (December to February): Naples and the Amalfi Coast's low season is the winter. Temperatures range from 8°C to 15°C (46°F to 59°F) due to the milder climate. The area has its own beauty in the winter, even though it might not be the finest time for beach activities. Naples' historic district may be explored, along with museums and archaeological sites, and local cuisine can be enjoyed. Prices are typically lower, and the ambience is less commercial and more authentic.

It's important to note that the Amalfi Coast can be busy throughout the year due to its popularity. If you prefer to avoid large crowds, consider visiting during the shoulder seasons of spring or autumn.

Ultimately, the best time to visit Naples and the Amalfi Coast depends on your preferences for weather, activities, and crowd levels. Consider these factors and choose a season that aligns with your interests and priorities.

What to pack

When packing for a trip to Naples and the Amalfi Coast, it's important to consider the Mediterranean climate and the activities you plan to engage in. Here's a suggested list of clothes and other travel necessities:

- Pack lightweight, breathable clothing that is appropriate for the current temperature. Choose textiles that are breathable, like cotton or linen. T-shirts, shorts, skirts, sundresses, and light slacks are all appropriate.
- Pack your swimsuit so you may take advantage of the opportunity to visit the stunning beaches and coastal surroundings.
- Light layers: Even though it's usually pleasant, it can get chilly in the nights, especially near the ocean. If necessary, bring a thin sweater or jacket to layer over your clothes.
- Bring appropriate walking shoes because you'll probably be touring the city streets, historical landmarks, and coastline pathways. The appropriate footwear is a sturdy pair of sneakers or sandals.
- Sun protection: To shield yourself from the sun's damaging UV rays, pack sunglasses, a hat, and sunscreen. The sun can be very strong in this area.
- Bring a beach towel, a beach bag, and a cover-up when you go to the beach. For added comfort, think about bringing a small inflatable pillow or beach mat.
- Even if it rains less frequently in the summer, it's still a good idea to carry an umbrella or a lightweight rain jacket with you at all times.
- A modest daypack or tote bag will be useful for carrying your necessities while you are touring the area.

- Check the electrical outlets in Italy before traveling, and bring a power adapter if necessary. Bring chargers for your electronic devices as well.
- Passport, travel insurance, photo identification, and any other required travel documents should not be forgotten. Also keeping copies of them in a different location is a smart idea.
- Basic amenities like a toothbrush, toothpaste, shampoo, and conditioner should also be packed, as well as any necessary prescriptions in their original packaging. Don't forget to abide by the liquid restrictions set by the airline.
- Consider carrying maps or guidebooks to help you explore and learn more about the area.

Remember to check the specific weather forecast for your travel dates and customize your packing list accordingly. Also, pack a mix of casual and slightly dressier outfits if you plan to visit any upscale restaurants or attend special events.

Getting there and moving around

To get to Naples and the Amalfi Coast, you have several transportation options available. Here's a guide on how to reach the region and move around once you're there:

1. Getting to Naples:
   - Naples International Airport is the closest international airport to the city (NAP). Numerous airlines offer nonstop flights from significant European cities to Naples. To get to your destination from the airport, you can either take a taxi or utilize public transportation.

- Naples has excellent train connections to other Italian towns. Naples can be reached by train from Rome, Florence, or other significant cities. Depending on the beginning site, the length of the voyage varies.
- Via bus: Long-distance buses connect Naples with a number of Italian cities.

2. Moving around Naples:
   - Naples boasts a sophisticated public transit system that includes buses, trams, and a metro. Tickets can be purchased from vending machines or kiosks and validated once you board the aircraft.
   - In Naples, taxis are widely available. They are available at designated taxi stands, or you can reserve one using a trustworthy taxi app.
   - Walking: Naples' old city center is rather small, so getting to know it on foot is a terrific opportunity to explore its winding streets and attractions.

3. Exploring the Amalfi Coast:
   - By train: Sorrento is a popular place to begin exploring the Amalfi Coast, and you can get there from Naples by taking a regional train. It takes an hour or so to travel by rail. You can continue your journey by bus or ferry from Sorrento.
   - By bus: Buses connect cities including Sorrento, Positano, Amalfi, and Ravello along the Amalfi Coast. Although the bus routes have beautiful scenery, they can get busy, especially during the busiest times of year.
   - By ferry: Ferries and hydrofoils connect coastal cities like Naples, Sorrento, Positano, and Amalfi. You can get beautiful views of the coastline and the Gulf of Naples by taking a ferry.

4. Moving around the Amalfi Coast:

- Buses: It is simple to get between towns thanks to the SITA bus company's extensive bus network along the Amalfi Coast. Tickets for buses can be purchased in advance or once on board.
- Taxis: Although they can be pricey, taxis are accessible in seaside communities. Prior to the trip, it is a good idea to check the rates or bargain with the driver.
- Strolling: For those who prefer trekking and soaking in the views, walking between villages or along the beach is a popular alternative along the Amalfi Coast.

The local transit schedules should always be checked because they can change based on the time of year. The Amalfi Coast can often get congested during the busiest travel seasons, so make your plans accordingly.

Practical Information for visitors

Language and Communication.

When visiting Naples and the Amalfi Coast in Italy, it is helpful to have some information about the language and communication in the region. Here are a few key points to keep in mind:

1. Language: The official language of Italy is Italian. While English is widely spoken in tourist areas, especially in hotels, restaurants, and shops, it is still a good idea to learn a few basic Italian phrases and expressions. The locals appreciate the effort and it can enhance your overall experience. Here are some essential phrases:

- Hello: Ciao (chow)
- Good morning: Buongiorno (bwon-jor-no)

- Good evening: Buonasera (bwon-a-se-ra)
- Please: Per favore (per fa-vo-re)
- Thank you: Grazie (gra-tsee-e)
- Yes: Sì (see)
- No: No (no)
- Excuse me: Scusa (scoo-za) / Scusate (scoo-za-te) (formal/plural)
- Do you speak English?: Parli inglese? (par-lee een-gleh-seh)

2. English Proficiency: In popular tourist areas, such as Naples and the Amalfi Coast, you'll find that many people, especially those in hospitality, tourism, and younger generations, speak English to varying degrees. However, it's always polite to begin a conversation with a greeting in Italian and then inquire about English.

3. Use of Gestures: Italians are known for their expressive gestures. While verbal communication is important, locals may also use hand gestures to convey their messages. Pay attention to non-verbal cues to enhance your understanding.

4. Phrasebooks and Translation Apps: Carrying a phrasebook or having a translation app on your smartphone can be handy if you encounter language barriers. These resources can assist you in translating specific words or phrases on the go.

5. Politeness and Courtesy: Italians appreciate politeness and courtesy. It's customary to greet people with a smile and a "buongiorno" or "buonasera" before starting a conversation. Remember to say "per favore" (please) and "grazie" (thank you) when interacting with locals.

6. Cultural Sensitivity: When visiting a foreign country, it's important to be respectful of local customs and culture.

Familiarize yourself with the local norms and practices to ensure that your communication is culturally appropriate.

7. Local Dialects: In Naples and surrounding areas, you may come across regional dialects such as Neapolitan. While Italian is the standard language, locals might use dialect among themselves. However, you can usually communicate effectively in standard Italian.

Money and banking

The euro (€) is the official unit of currency in Italy. For modest purchases, it is good to have some euros on hand, especially in rural areas or tiny businesses that might not accept credit cards.

ATMs: Both Naples and the Amalfi Coast have plenty of ATMs, often known as "Bancomat" in Italy. They can be discovered anywhere in the cities and towns, including banks, train stations, and airports. Most ATMs offer instructions in several languages and accept the most popular debit and credit cards from around the world. Remember that some ATMs may impose a cost for withdrawals, and your bank might impose foreign transaction fees as well.

Credit Cards: In Naples and the Amalfi Coast, the majority of hotels, eateries, and bigger retail establishments take credit cards including Visa, Mastercard, and American Express. However, it's always a good idea to have some cash on hand, especially when visiting smaller businesses or more distant locations where card acceptance may be scarce.

Currency Exchange: At banks and currency exchange offices, you can exchange foreign currencies for euros. Banks often have competitive rates, however their hours of operation may be restricted. The hours of exchange offices in well-known tourist places may be more flexible, but their prices might be a little worse. Before exchanging money, it is advised to compare exchange rates and charges.

Traveler's checks may not be accepted by many Italian establishments because they aren't as commonly utilized as they formerly were. Generally speaking, using credit cards and ATM withdrawals of cash is more practical.

Banking Hours: Banks in Italy usually have regular business hours from 8:30 AM to 1:30 PM, Monday through Friday. In the afternoon, some of the larger branches can reopen for a few hours. The fact that banks are closed on weekends and federal holidays should not be overlooked.

Safety information

When visiting Naples and the Amalfi Coast, it's essential to prioritize your safety to have a pleasant and secure experience. Here are some safety tips and information for visitors:

- Pickpocketing should be avoided at all costs. Be especially watchful in busy areas, on public transportation, and at tourist attractions. Use a money belt or a covert bag to keep your stuff secure.
- Use safe modes of transportation: When utilizing taxis, pick reputed, licensed firms or ask your hotel for a recommendation. Using authorized taxi stands is preferable to hailing a cab at random from the street. Keep a watch on your valuables because the buses and metro in Naples can get crowded.

- Stay vigilant and aware of your surroundings, especially in congested places or popular tourist destinations. Be wary of people acting strangely or diversions. Consider staying in busy, well-lit locations rather than remote or dimly lighted areas at night.
- When visiting religious sites or more traditional locations, it is especially essential to dress modestly. Naples and the Amalfi Coast are generally laid-back destinations. Avoid wearing skimpy clothing or beachwear in areas that aren't on the beach to show respect for the local culture and customs.
- Be careful with valuables: Refrain from openly exhibiting pricey jewelry, cameras, or electronics as this may draw unwelcome attention. Carry your possessions in discrete bags, and think about storing valuables in a safe deposit box at your lodging when not in use.
- Keep yourself hydrated and use sunscreen when visiting the Amalfi Coast in the summer when temperatures can soar. To avoid sunburns and other heat-related problems, stay hydrated by drinking plenty of water, using sunscreen, and using suitable sun protection.
- Employ licensed tour operators: If you intend to go on excursions or guided tours along the Amalfi Coast, make sure the tour operators you choose are reliable and authorized. To ensure a secure and dependable experience, check reviews and suggestions in advance.
- Observe COVID-19 recommendations: Keep up with Naples' and the Amalfi Coast's most recent COVID-19 rules and regulations. Pay attention to any instructions provided by local health officials during your visit on

the wearing of masks, maintaining a distance from others, and other matters.

- When driving, exercise caution: Coastal roads along the Amalfi Coast can be congested, winding, and difficult to drive on if you decide to rent a car and travel there. Drive carefully, obey the regulations of the road, and if you feel uncomfortable driving under these circumstances, think about taking the bus or hiring a driver from the area.
- Research and preparation Investigate the places you intend to visit in advance, taking note of any potential security issues or recent changes. Keep up with any travel advice or cautions that your embassy or consulate may issue.

Chapter 2:
Must Visit Places in Naples and Amalfi Coast.

Exploring Naples

Naples, the third-most populous city in Italy, serves as the regional capital of Campania. It is the second-largest metropolitan region after Milan.

Napoli welcomes travelers each year to see its beauty and wealth thanks to its typical mild Mediterranean climate and ideal location sandwiched between Campi Flegrei and Vesuvius. They can explore the alleys of this historic town and take in the palaces, castles, basilicas, and churches that give the area its mystique.

Naples boasts many historical sites, restaurants serving local cuisine, and fantastic tourist attractions. Naples is a strange city with an almost mathematical layout thanks to the historic city structure that has been retained. Naples welcomes you to take a leisurely stroll along the numerous sites of mythology with its three parallel main streets and various cross streets.

The Greeks founded the city, which they called Neapolis, which means "new city," between the seventh and sixth centuries BC. The ancient center of Naples was included to the UNESCO World Cultural History list in 1995 due to its extensive artistic heritage. The city is home to 448 historic churches, the most in a single city and one of the greatest historical centers in the world.

Naples has long served as a hub for commercial routes in the Mediterranean and a meeting point for various cultural groups. This history is mirrored in the city and its people; there are numerous impressive museums, cathedrals, and monuments to be found here.

Every traveler will undoubtedly discover something interesting: Great painters' paintings and sculptures, opulent royal rooms furnished with antiques, subterranean Roman city excavations, imposing cathedrals, and modest churches.

Attractions

1. Naples National Archaeological Museum

Naples National Archaeological Museum, located in Naples, Italy, is a treasure trove of ancient artifacts and archaeological discoveries. As a tourist, visiting this museum provides a unique opportunity to explore the rich history of Naples and the surrounding region. Here are some tourist highlights and activities, including a few hidden gems, that you can enjoy during your visit:

- Farnese Collection: One of the center pieces of the museum is the Farnese Collection. Along with other fine marble statues and historic Roman artwork, it contains the well-known Farnese Bull, a huge Roman sculpture. The splendor of the Roman Empire can be seen in this collection.

- Pompeii and Herculaneum Artifacts: The neighboring ancient cities of Pompeii and Herculaneum, which were destroyed by the eruption of Mount Vesuvius in 79 AD, are represented in the museum by a sizable collection of items. You can be in awe of the dexterous mosaics, frescoes, sculptures, and commonplace items that reveal details about the daily life of the people who once inhabited these towns.

- Secret Cabinet (Gabinetto Segreto): One of the museum's hidden gems is The Secret Cabinet. It has a variety of antique erotic artwork and artifacts from Herculaneum and Pompeii. It offers a distinctive viewpoint on the private lives and sexual customs of the ancient Romans, albeit it might not be appropriate for all visitors.

- Egyptian Collection: The museum also has a noteworthy collection of Egyptian artifacts, including mummies, sarcophagi, and other ancient Egyptian relics. You can delve into the fascinating realm of the gods, pharaohs, and rituals from ancient Egypt.

- Farnese Hercules: The Farnese Hercules, a monumental marble statue of the mythical hero Hercules, is another noteworthy attraction. Art lovers must see this treasure since it displays the outstanding craftsmanship of ancient sculptors.

- Temporary Exhibitions: Temporary exhibitions with an emphasis on particular themes or eras are frequently held at the museum. These displays offer more information on several facets of ancient history and archaeology. Check the museum's calendar to see if any special exhibitions are scheduled to run while you are there.
- Garden of the Fugitives: The Garden of the Fugitives, a recreation of a garden from the ancient city of Pompeii, lies next to the museum. It includes plaster replicas of the volcanic eruption victims, captured in their death moments. This moving exhibit serves as a somber reminder of Pompeii's catastrophe.
- Villa of the Papyri: An exact reproduction of the ancient Roman villa known as the Villa of the Papyri, which was destroyed by Mount Vesuvius' explosion, is kept in the museum. The mansion was renowned for its extraordinary collection of papyrus scrolls, and the facsimile offers an impression of its opulence.
- Mosaic Collection: A collection of stunning old mosaics is hidden inside the museum. Visitors frequently pass by these exquisite works of art, which demonstrate the remarkable craftsmanship of the Roman era.
- Cabinet of the Philosophers: A collection of busts and pictures of prominent ancient philosophers and intellectuals can be found in this little museum area. It provides a serene setting for contemplation of the ancient world's intellectual and philosophical legacy.
- Virtual Reality Experience: Try the virtual reality tour that the museum offers for a distinctive and engaging experience. It gives you the opportunity to digitally

tour Pompeii's ruins, bringing the ancient city to life before your very eyes.

- Terrace and Panoramic Views: A rooftop patio at the museum offers breath-taking panoramas of Naples and Mount Vesuvius. Enjoy a coffee or snack from the museum café while taking some time to unwind and take in the surroundings.

Guided Tours and Workshops: Consider taking a tour with a guide or taking part in a class at the museum to make the most of your visit. In-depth explanations of the exhibits can be given by knowledgeable interpreters, and workshops allow opportunities for hands-on activities like producing pottery or learning historical painting techniques.

2. Castel dell'Ovo

A spectacular medieval castle called Castel dell'Ovo may be seen near Naples, Italy. It is placed on a tiny island called Megaride in the Gulf of Naples. As a tourist, discovering Castel dell'Ovo offers a fascinating look into the city's lengthy history as well as a variety of attractions and enjoyable activities. Let's explore the castle's tourist destinations and undiscovered gems.

- Historical Importance: Castel dell'Ovo, which dates to the 12th century, is one of Naples's oldest remaining defences. It has been a part of history for centuries, including the Byzantine, Norman, and Angevin dynasties. You can immerse yourself in the castle's rich past by exploring it.
- Views: From the castle, visitors may enjoy breathtaking panoramas of Naples, the Gulf, and the surrounding countryside. You can take in the breathtaking skyline, the charming harbor, and the recognizable Vesuvius volcano from its ramparts and terraces. It's a great location for shooting pictures and admiring the splendor of the city.
- Museum of Prehistory: Located inside of Castel dell'Ovo, the Museum of Prehistory is home to an impressive collection of antiquities from the Paleolithic, Neolithic, and Bronze Ages. You can find relics from the Roman era as well as old tools and ceramics. This museum provides a window into the region's ancient civilizations.
- Marina and Seaside Promenade: The castle is perched on a promontory, and a picturesque marina and a seaside promenade may be found nearby. Take a stroll down the waterfront to enjoy the vibrant scene, the crisp sea wind, and the cafés and eateries. It's the perfect spot to unwind and observe folks.
- Concerts & Events: Throughout the year, Castel dell'Ovo holds a number of concerts and cultural events. These occasions include everything from classical music concerts to exhibitions of modern

artwork. To make the most of your stay and to fully immerse yourself in the local culture, check the local calendar to see if any events are scheduled to take place while you are there..

Hidden Gems:

- Borgo Marinari: Borgo Marinari is a charming fishing village located close to Castel dell'Ovo. This hidden treasure provides a peaceful retreat from the busy metropolis with its winding streets, vibrant homes, and charming seafood eateries. While dining on delicious seafood meals, take in the picturesque setting.
- Grotta di Seiano: Below the castle, in the tuff rock, is a network of old tunnels known as the Grotta di Seiano. Throughout history, these tunnels were employed for communication and defense purposes. Today, you may explore this intriguing maze as part of guided excursions that reveal the castle's hidden past.

3. Naples Underground

Exploring Naples Underground in Naples can be a fascinating experience for tourists. The city is known for its rich history and intricate network of tunnels, catacombs, and caves that lie beneath its surface. Here are some tourist highlights and activities, including hidden gems, that you can discover in Naples Underground:

- One of Naples' top tourist destinations is the Napoli Sotterranea (Naples Underground). A maze of tunnels, chambers, and aqueducts from the Greek and Roman eras are explored in guided excursions. The history of the city will be shown to you, together with ancient antiquities and even a Roman theater that has been buried beneath contemporary streets.
- The catacombs of San Gennaro are a mysterious but fascinating location to explore. They are situated in the northern portion of the city. They have frescoes from the second century AD and early Christian graveyards. The veneration of San Gennaro, Naples' patron saint, and early Christian history are both shown in the catacombs.

- The underground Bourbon Tunnel, also known as the Galleria Borbonica, was constructed as the royal family's escape route. The tunnel is now open to the public as part of guided tours that highlight its historical value and give historical context for the area. During World War II, the tunnel also used as a bunker.
- Crypta Neapolitana: This historic tunnel, which dates to the fourth century BC, is one of the oldest in Naples. It was built initially as an aqueduct and later utilized as a burial ground. The tunnel can be explored by visitors, who can also view its magnificent architecture and niches that originally housed sarcophagi.
- While the basilica itself is a striking structure, it also provides access to a distinctive underground archaeological site. Explore the remains of old Roman structures, including as a market, hot baths, and a macellum, that are located beneath the church (meat market). The archaeological site gives visitors a look into daily life in prehistoric Naples.
- Visit the underground market in Naples for a unique shopping experience. It is located close to Piazza San Gaetano. Numerous stores and stalls selling typical Neapolitan products, including food, crafts, and mementos, can be found here. It's a fantastic location to learn about regional goods and experience Naples' energetic atmosphere.
- Residence of the Vettii This Pompeii-based ancient Roman residence features amazingly preserved frescoes, mosaics, and architectural details. Although it is not immediately beneath Naples, it is close by and offers a look at ordinary life in ancient Rome.
- The Cistern of the Aqueduct is a hidden treasure in the Materdei neighborhood that provides a singular

underground experience. It is a sizable cistern that was constructed in the Roman era to hold water for the city. The location is currently accessible to the general public, allowing guests to explore the tunnels and chambers below..

4. Naples Cathedral(duomo)

Naples Cathedral, also known as the Duomo, is a must-visit tourist attraction in Naples, Italy. This impressive cathedral has a rich history and offers visitors a fascinating blend of architectural beauty, religious significance, and cultural treasures. Let's explore the highlights and activities you can enjoy while visiting Naples Cathedral, including some hidden gems.

- Naples Cathedral is a beautiful example of the fusion of Gothic, Renaissance, and Baroque architectural styles. Complex sculptures, colorful frescoes, and a stunning central rose window decorate its façade. The interior is equally stunning, featuring magnificent chapels, massive domes, and delicate marble work. Spend some time admiring the cathedral's exquisite details and craftsmanship.

- Chapel of the Treasure of San Gennaro: The Chapel of the Treasure of San Gennaro is one of Naples Cathedral's most notable features. The blood vials and relics of San Gennaro, the patron saint of Naples, are kept in this church. The vials are reported to mysteriously liquefy during the elaborate ceremonies done three times a year. The chapel also showcases magnificent artwork, priceless jewels, and sacred objects.
- Baptistry of San Giovanni in Fonte: The Baptistry of San Giovanni in Fonte is located close to the cathedral. One of the world's oldest Christian baptisteries, this historic structure dates to the fourth century. Admire the architectural features and mosaics that have been carefully conserved and that offer a look into Naples' early Christian history.
- A unique collection of religious artwork and antiques can be found at the Museo del Tesoro di San Gennaro (Treasury Museum), which is a part of the cathedral complex. Explore the museum to see amazing statues, jewelry, silverware, paintings, and other priceless items. The museum provides insights into Naples' rich religious and cultural legacy.
- Climb the Bell Tower: Ascend the bell tower of the cathedral for sweeping views over Naples. The reward is well worth it even though the ascent could be a little difficult. You can take in breath-taking panoramas of the cityscape, including views of Mount Vesuvius and

the Bay of Naples, from the summit. For those who love taking pictures, it's a great opportunity.

Hidden Gems:

- Crypt of San Gennaro: The Crypt of San Gennaro is a hidden treasure that many visitors frequently overlook. It is located beneath the cathedral. There are several frescoes and mosaics in this old underground chamber, which is thought to be San Gennaro's ultimate resting place. Discover the crypt's historical and aesthetic treasures by exploring it.
- Don't miss the early Christian chapel known as the Chapel of Santa Restituta, which is located inside the cathedral complex and predates the cathedral itself. Beautiful Byzantine paintings, antiquated columns, and a subterranean archaeological site are all present. This undiscovered treasure offers a window into Naples's early Christian past.
- Diocesan Museum: Although it's not a part of the cathedral itself, the close-by Diocesan Museum is well worth a trip for art lovers. It holds a magnificent collection of paintings, sculptures, and religious items from the medieval and Renaissance periods. The museum provides a more sedate and private setting for appreciating the local artistic legacy.

Exploring Naples Cathedral (Duomo) in Naples is an enriching experience that combines history, art, and spirituality. From the architectural marvels to the hidden gems, this cathedral offers a captivating journey through Naples' cultural tapestry.

5. Spaccanapoli

Tourists may find it exciting and educational to explore Spaccanapoli in Naples. Spaccanapoli, a lengthy and winding street that divides Naples' old town into two sections, provides a window into the city's thriving culture, extensive history, and stunning architectural treasures. The following are some tourist attractions and things to do while in Spaccanapoli:

- San Gregorio Armeno: San Gregorio Armeno is a well-known street where you can begin your tour. It is recognized for its artisan workshops that produce presepi (Nativity scenes). Particularly during the Christmas season, you may see experienced artisans crafting exquisite figurines and decorations here.
- Even though San Domenico Maggiore is frequently overshadowed by the nearby Naples Cathedral, it is nonetheless worthwhile to visit. Awe-inspiring marble statues may be seen in the Chapel of San Severo, a particular highlight of the interior.
- Explore the Via dei Tribunali, one of Naples's oldest and liveliest neighborhoods, and its winding lanes. Classic pizzerias, real trattorias, neighborhood markets, and stores that sell sfogliatelle and other traditional Neapolitan sweets may all be found here.
- Pio Monte della Misericordia: The famous work by Caravaggio, "The Seven Works of Mercy," is housed in this less well-known museum. Spend some time admiring this magnificent picture and perusing the other works of art and historical objects on show.
- Napoli Sotterranea (Subterranean Naples): Explore Napoli Sotterranea, a system of tunnels, caverns, and secret areas, to delve even deeper into Naples'

underground. Discover mysterious tunnels, historic aqueducts, and intriguing archaeological ruins by taking a guided tour.

- Visit the medieval church of San Lorenzo Maggiore, which is located above Roman remains, to travel back in time. Discover the historical layers that make up Naples' complicated history as you explore the underground archaeological area.
- Discover the tranquil Santa Chiara Monastery, which is renowned for its stunning cloister decorated with vibrant majolica tiles. Explore the complex's tranquil garden, church, and archaeological museum.

6. Capodimonte Museum

The Capodimonte Museum in Naples is a fantastic destination for art enthusiasts and history lovers. Located in the beautiful Capodimonte Park, this museum is home to an impressive collection of Italian and European art spanning several centuries. Let's explore some of the tourist highlights, activities, and hidden gems that make a visit to the Capodimonte Museum truly memorable.

- The museum has a wide collection of artworks, including decorative arts, sculptures, and paintings. The paintings by well-known artists including Caravaggio, Titian, Botticelli, Raphael, and many others are among the highlights. The collection provides a thorough survey of Italian art history.
- Don't miss the opportunity to visit the Royal Apartments as you tour the museum. The Naples Bourbon kings previously resided in these opulently adorned halls. Admire the lavish decor, ornate

tapestries, and stunning frescoes that take you back in time.

- The Farnese Collection is one of the Capodimonte Museum's undiscovered treasures. Many of the sculptures, paintings, and artifacts in this collection are ancient Roman creations that were unearthed nearby in the Herculaneum and Pompeii archaeological sites. It offers a remarkable window into the ancient Roman world's art and culture.
- Capodimonte Park: The expansive Capodimonte Park surrounds the museum and provides a tranquil respite from the bustle of the city. Take a leisurely stroll in the park, take in the beautiful scenery, and discover a quiet place to unwind in the midst of nature.
- Temporary Exhibitions: The museum frequently presents transient displays that highlight various subjects and artistic disciplines. These exhibits provide novel viewpoints and chances to learn about lesser-known artists or artistic movements.
- Cafés & Restaurants: The museum has cafés and restaurants where you may stop for a bite to eat or a cup of coffee if you need a break from touring. Spend some time enjoying the local cuisine and taking in the atmosphere.
- Panoramic Views: For sweeping views of Naples, visit the museum's terrace or garden. You may take in the breathtaking views of the ancient district, Mount Vesuvius, and the Bay of Naples from here.
- Events, Seminars, and Lectures: The Capodimonte Museum routinely hosts lectures, workshops, and cultural gatherings. If you want to participate in any events during your visit that match your interests,

check their schedule. These occasions may provide fascinating insights into the local and art worlds.

Consider hiring a guide or audio guide to provide you in-depth knowledge about the artworks and the history of the Capodimonte Museum so that you can get the most out of your visit. You will undoubtedly have a great appreciation for art, culture, and history after exploring this Naples hidden gem.

7. Sansevero Chapel

The Sansevero Chapel, located in Naples, Italy, is a fascinating tourist destination renowned for its stunning art and architecture. Let's explore the highlights and activities you can enjoy during your visit, including some hidden gems.

1. Admire the Veiled Christ: The Veiled Christ is one of the Sansevero Chapel's most well-known features (Cristo Velato). The transparent marble veil that covers Christ's torso in this Giuseppe Sanmartino masterwork is painstakingly carved to mimic the texture and nuances of the cloth. It is a magnificent work of baroque art.
2. Take a look at the anatomical machines: The Anatomical Machines, a collection of preserved human anatomical specimens, is another distinctive aspect of the Sansevero Chapel. Giuseppe Salerno, a physician and scientist, developed these detailed models that offer a look at the internal organs of the human body.
3. Examine the Architecture of the Chapel: The chapel itself is a unique architectural marvel in addition to its artistic treasures. Admire the interior's opulent furnishings, elaborate murals, and exquisite marble

columns. Baroque and Rococo themes are flawlessly incorporated into the chapel's architecture.

4. Discover the hidden gems:

- The Chapel of the Prince: Located within the Sansevero Chapel complex, the Chapel of the Prince (Cappella del Principe) is often overlooked by visitors. It features beautiful marble sculptures and an imposing funerary monument dedicated to the family of Raimondo di Sangro, the chapel's founder.
- The Masonic Symbols: Look closely, and you'll find intriguing Masonic symbols hidden within the artwork of the chapel. Raimondo di Sangro, who was a Freemason, incorporated these symbols subtly into the chapel's decoration, adding an extra layer of mystery and intrigue.
- The Globe with Veins: In a small room adjacent to the main chapel, you'll discover the Globe with Veins (Globo con Vene). This striking sculpture represents the interconnectedness of all knowledge and features a series of intricate blood vessels carved into a white marble sphere.

5. Attend Cultural Events: Throughout the year, the Sansevero Chapel also holds a number of cultural events, including musical performances and art exhibits. If there are any special activities scheduled during your visit, check the schedule to see if you may take advantage of the chance to see the chapel from a different perspective.

8. Santa Chiara Complex

The Santa Chiara Complex in Naples, Italy, is a popular tourist destination known for its historical significance and architectural beauty. Here's a discussion of the highlights and activities you can enjoy while exploring this complex, including some hidden gems.

- Santa Chiara Church: The Santa Chiara Church, a spectacular specimen of Gothic architecture, serves as the complex's focal point. The church, which was built in the fourteenth century, is renowned for the vivid blue majolica tiles that decorate the cloister.
- One of the primary attractions in the complex is the Cloister of the Clarisses. There are beautiful flowers and a courtyard with colorful tile work. Admire the stunning architectural elements as you meander leisurely along the cloister.
- Located inside the complex, the Museum of the Treasure of San Gennaro is home to a magnificent collection of religious artwork and priceless artifacts, including the jewels and relics of San Gennaro, the patron saint of Naples. Discover the history and customs connected to the city's patron saint by exploring the museum.
- The Santa Chiara Complex also has an archaeological region where the ruins of the Baths of Queen Giovanna, a Roman thermal bath complex, are preserved. Investigate this area to see examples of the lifestyle and architecture of the Roman Empire.
- Capella del Crocefisso: Tourists frequently overlook this tiny chapel since it is hidden away within the complex. It features amazing wooden crucifix and lovely frescoes. Visit this undiscovered treasure and savor the minute details.

- The Majolica Cloister, sometimes referred to as the Chiostro delle Ceramiche, is located next to the main cloister. A remarkable collection of hand-painted ceramic tiles with elaborate designs, illustrating biblical themes and historical events, may be found in this less well-known neighborhood.
- Outdoor Terrace: After seeing the building, head outside to the terrace to take in the expansive views of Naples and Mount Vesuvius. Enjoy the serene ambience of the complex while taking in the gorgeous scenery.
- Cultural Events: The Santa Chiara Complex frequently offers cultural activities like musical performances, art exhibits, and theatrical productions. Immerse yourself in the thriving cultural scene by checking the schedule to see if any events are scheduled to take place while you are there.
- Shopping in the Monastic Shop: Before you leave, be sure to stop by the complex's on-site Monastic Shop. Gourmet foods, handcrafted soaps, and religious mementos are just a few of the local goods that monks and nuns produce here.

9. Vomero District

The Vomero district in Naples, Italy, is a vibrant and charming neighborhood that offers a mix of historical landmarks, stunning views, and local culture. As a tourist, there are several highlights and activities worth exploring in Vomero, including some hidden gems. Let's delve into them:

- Castel Sant'Elmo: The Castel Sant'Elmo is one of Vomero's most recognizable landmarks. From this ancient fortress, you can see all of Naples and its surroundings. The interior of the castle is open for exploration, and you may go to the museum of contemporary art and take in the magnificent views from its walls.
- The Certosa e Museo di San Martino is a former monastery that currently serves as a museum, and it is close to Castel Sant'Elmo. The museum displays works of art from Naples, historical objects, and provides information about the city's religious history. The monastery's beautiful gardens and architectural design add to its allure.
- Villa Floridiana: In the center of Vomero, this lovely park is a peaceful haven. It has breathtaking views of the Bay of Naples, as well as luxuriant foliage and vibrant flowers. Enjoy a leisurely stroll, a picnic, or a trip to the park's tiny art gallery.
- San Gennaro is the patron saint of Naples, and this church honors him. It is located in the Capodimonte neighborhood of Vomero. Beautiful frescoes and sculptures embellish the church's baroque interior. Don't pass up the opportunity to see the liquefaction of San Gennaro's blood, which occurs twice a year.
- Antignano Market: Visit the Antignano Market for a truly local experience. This crowded street market sells

an assortment of fresh fruit, regional delicacies, and distinctive goods. Enjoy the lively ambiance, chat with the welcoming sellers, and indulge in some authentic Neapolitan sweets.

- Palazzo dello Spagnolo: This hidden gem is tucked away in a small alley and is worth finding. A cultural center now resides in this palace from the sixteenth century, which accommodates exhibitions, musical performances, and other artistic events. To find out if there will be any performances when you are there, check their schedule.
- Parco della Rimembranza: Visit Parco della Rimembranza if you're looking for a beautiful place to stroll. The Mediterranean Sea, Mount Vesuvius, and Naples are all visible from this park's vantage point. It's the ideal location for unwinding, taking in the sunset, and taking beautiful pictures.
- Vomero's "Giardini Segreti," also known as the "Secret Gardens," are a collection of obscured green areas nestled away behind the city's structures. These serene gardens provide a much-needed respite from the busy city. Enjoy the peaceful surroundings while taking a break from sightseeing.
- Local cuisine and beverage options abound in Vomero, including quaint cafes, classic trattorias, and wine bars. Try traditional Neapolitan fare like the pizza margherita, pasta alla Genovese, and sfogliatelle pastries. Drink a glass of regional wine or the traditional liqueur, Limoncello, while enjoying your meal.
- Shopping on Via Scarlatti: In Vomero, Via Scarlatti is a busy street lined with shops, boutiques, and regional

craftspeople. Discover unusual items, browse the little shops, and get a taste of the neighborhood shopping.

10.   Catacombs of San Gaudioso

Tourists may find the Catacombs of San Gaudioso in Naples to be a fascinating and immersive experience. These historic underground burial chambers provide visitors a unique look into the city's culture and history. Here are some tourist hotspots and activities to take into account while you're there, including a few undiscovered gems:

- Historical Importance: The San Gaudioso Catacombs were utilized as a place of burial for early Christians, aristocrats, and simple people. They date back to the 5th century. The location is of tremendous historical and religious significance because it shows how early Christian activities developed from pagan Roman beliefs.
- Guided Tours: It is advised to take a guided tour in order to properly understand the historical and cultural significance of the catacombs. Knowledgeable tour guides will give in-depth explanations, anecdotes, and insights on the history, architecture, and individuals interred at the site.
- Visit the San Gaudioso Basilica, a stunning cathedral that complements the underground location, which is close to the catacombs. The basilica offers a contrast to the solemn atmosphere of the catacombs by showcasing magnificent religious artwork and beautiful murals.
- Artistic Remains: The catacombs contain well preserved mosaics, frescoes, and sculptures that

showcase the period's skill and talent. These works of art offer a singular window into historical religious and cultural views.

- The neighboring Capella Sansevero is a hidden gem that is worth investigating even if it is not immediately connected to the Catacombs of San Gaudioso. Along with other remarkable works of art, it is home to the well-known Veiled Christ sculpture, which is regarded as a masterpiece of marble sculpture.

- Various underground crypts that contain the remains of people from various socioeconomic classes can be found as you explore the catacombs. The social hierarchy of the crypts provides an intriguing viewpoint on the burial practices and social structure of the era.

- Sacred Soil Chapel: The Sacred Soil Chapel is a distinctive aspect of the catacombs. Jars containing soil from the Holy Land that pilgrims carried back as a sign of their devotion can be found here. The area is calm and introspective, which enhances the site's spiritual atmosphere.

- Catacombs of San Gennaro: If you have a special interest in catacomb exploration, you should think about visiting the neighboring Catacombs of San Gennaro. These catacombs provide a unique experience because to their magnificent murals, historical connections to Naples' patron saint, and ancient tombs.

11. Villa Pignatelli

Villa Pignatelli is a beautiful historic villa located in Naples, Italy. As a tourist, you'll find plenty of highlights and activities to enjoy during your visit. From its stunning architecture to hidden gems, here's a discussion on exploring Villa Pignatelli and what it has to offer:

1. Architecture of Villa Pignatelli: The villa itself is a work of art, fusing Romantic and Neoclassical features. It was constructed in the 19th century and features ornate façade, elaborate decorations, and lovely gardens.

2. Museo Principe Diego Aragona Pignatelli Cortes, a museum featuring a variety of art collections, is located in Villa Pignatelli today. Explore the interior's numerous rooms to see the china, paintings, sculptures, antique furniture, and decorative arts. The museum offers information on Naples's past and present.

3. Gardens and Property: The villa is surrounded by lush grounds that provide a tranquil escape from the busy metropolis. Enjoy a leisurely stroll through the well-kept gardens, breathe in the scent of the blossoming flowers, and unwind on seats while you take in the statues and fountains that are dotted all over.

4. Villa Pignatelli frequently presents transient exhibitions that feature modern art, photography, or other cultural displays. These exhibits offer a chance to interact with contemporary interpretations in a historical environment.

5. Hidden Gems in Villa Pignatelli:
   - The Grotto: A lovely underground grotto is one of Villa Pignatelli's best-kept secrets. This wonderful location has stalactites, a calm environment, and tiny waterfalls. It's the ideal place to get out of the heat and spend some time in an unusual underground setting.

- Don't pass up the chance to check out the villa's opulent tea room. This elaborate salon provides a window into the affluent way of living in the past. While surrounded by stunning frescoes and antique furniture, sip tea or coffee.
- The Terrace: The terrace of the home offers sweeping views of the Gulf of Naples. It's the perfect place to unwind, take pictures, and take in the breathtaking views of the area, including the adjacent Castel dell'Ovo and Mount Vesuvius.
- The Chapel: A tiny chapel that hosts religious services is located on the villa's grounds. Exploring the chapel's structure and religious artwork will give you a better understanding of the villa's spiritual past.

12. Palazzo dello Spagnolo

The Palace of the Spaniard, sometimes referred to as Palazzo dello Spagnolo, is a significant historical site in Naples, Italy. This magnificent palace, which was constructed in the 16th century, draws visitors from all over the world because of its significant historical and cultural heritage. Let's look at the attractions and things to do at Palazzo dello Spagnolo, including some undiscovered gems.

- Historical Significance: Entering Palazzo dello Spagnolo will transport you to Naples under the Spanish occupation. The palace features stunning Renaissance-era architectural features and was once built as a home for the Spanish viceroy.
- The palace has beautiful architecture, with a huge courtyard, arches, and elaborate embellishments.

You'll find stunning frescoes, dexterous stucco work, and lovely tapestries within that capture the wealth of the time.

- Museum: The Museum of the Neapolitan Art of the 18th Century, which houses a great collection of works from the Neapolitan School, is located in Palazzo dello Spagnolo. Famous artists including Francesco Solimena, Giuseppe Bonito, and Francesco de Mura have produced works that can be admired.
- The Sala del Tesoro, also known as the Treasury Room, is one of the palace's secret treasures. An amazing collection of historic coins, medals, and priceless objects that shed light on Naples's economic significance and history are on exhibit in this chamber.
- Rooftop Terrace: Spend a minute ascending to the palace's rooftop terrace for expansive views of Naples. Enjoy the stunning views of the metropolis, which include famous sites like Mount Vesuvius, the Bay of Naples, and the historic center's roofs.
- Events and Exhibitions: The Palazzo dello Spagnolo frequently holds cultural activities like art exhibits, concerts, and workshops. If there are any special events happening while you are there, check the schedule.
- Guided Tours: Think about taking a guided tour to properly understand the significance and history of the Palazzo dello Spagnolo. Your journey will be made even more interesting by the knowledgeable experts' insightful explanations of the palace's architecture, artwork, and historical setting.
- Local Cuisine: After touring the palace, travel through the neighborhood of Naples to sample the city's world-famous cuisine. Try classic Neapolitan meals like

sfogliatelle, spaghetti alle vongole, and pizza Margherita (a delicious pastry).

Exploring Amalfi Coast

1. Amalfi Town

Begin your exploration in Amalfi itself.

Amalfi Town, a quaint and attractive town on Italy's breathtaking Amalfi Coast, is home to a variety of tourist attractions and activities. Everyone may find something to enjoy in Amalfi Town, whether they are interested in historical sites, spectacular natural beauty, or delectable regional food. Let's investigate the town's tourist hotspots and secret attractions.

Tourist Highlights in Amalfi Town:

- The majestic Amalfi Cathedral, also known as the Duomo di Amalfi, is the focal point of Amalfi Town. Explore the spectacular interior, which includes the Cloister of Paradise, and take in the remarkable architecture with Byzantine and Moorish influences.
- Amalfi's Old Town: Stroll through the lanes adorned with pastel-colored homes and charming boutiques that make up the old town. Visit picturesque piazzas, artisan shops, and delightful cafes to sample the pastries and coffee from the region.
- Valle dei Mulini: Take a leisurely stroll through this gorgeous valley, which is littered with the remains of former paper mills. Enjoy the serene atmosphere and the relaxing sound of waterfalls.
- Visit the thriving Amalfi Harbor to see fishing boats and opulent yachts come and go. Consider taking a boat cruise around the coast to see the stunning cliffs and undiscovered bays.
- Learn about Amalfi's famous paper-making industry at the Paper Museum (Museo della Carta). Learn about the traditional processes used to make lovely handmade paper and perhaps give it a shot.

Hidden Gems in Amalfi Town:

- Torre dello Ziro: Visit Torre dello Ziro for sweeping views of the coast and Amalfi. This historic watchtower provides an incredible vantage point and a chance to get away from the crowds.
- Villa Cimbrone Gardens: In the village of Ravello, not far from Amalfi Town, are the magnificent Villa Cimbrone Gardens. Discover the exquisitely kept

gardens, which are embellished with statues, fountains, and expansive terraces offering sea views.

- The spectacular sea cave known as the Emerald Grotto (Grotta dello Smeraldo), which is close to Amalfi, shines an emerald green color at night. Experience the magnificent atmosphere generated by the sunlight penetrating through the cave's underwater opening by taking a boat trip.
- Atrani: The lovely village of Atrani is only a short stroll from Amalfi Town. Explore its winding streets, take in the beauty of its medieval architecture, and take in a more tranquil ambiance away from the busy tourist crowds.
- Discover the remote splendor of Fiordo di Furore, a fjord-like bay tucked away amid imposing rocks. For a serene and picturesque experience, go swimming in the beautiful waters or simply unwind on the tiny beach.

2. Positano

Exploring Positano in the Amalfi Coast is a delightful experience for tourists, as this picturesque town offers a perfect blend of stunning landscapes, charming architecture, and a vibrant Mediterranean atmosphere. Let's dive into the tourist highlights and activities, including some hidden gems, that make Positano an unforgettable destination.

- Spiaggia Grande: Positano's main beach, Spiaggia Grande, is a bustling area where visitors can soak up the sun, go swimming in the clean seas, and take in the breathtaking views of the colorful homes that cascade over the cliffs.

- The Church of Santa Maria Assunta is a must-see attraction since it dominates the town's skyline. Explore its recognizable dome and magnificent medieval artwork, which includes the Byzantine icon of the Black Madonna.
- Path of the Gods: The magnificent Path of the Gods is a favorite destination for hikers (Sentiero degli Dei). The Amalfi Coast, with its towering cliffs and terraced vineyards, may be seen in its whole from this magnificent walk.
- Visit Marina Grande, a tiny fishing community within Positano, for a flavor of local life. Discover the city's picturesque beachfront, observe the fishermen bringing in their catch, and sample the local trattorias' fresh seafood.
- Fornillo Beach is a quieter, more seclusion-oriented area that is situated away from the busy Spiaggia Grande. Enjoy the quiet atmosphere and pebbly shoreline while surrounded by rich vegetation.
- Chiesa di San Gennaro: Uphill from the main town center, this tiny church provides a tranquil haven away from the bustle. From its courtyard, see the stunning architecture and take in the expansive views of Positano.
- Cooking classes: Enroll in a cooking lesson to fully experience Positano's gastronomic offerings. Day Trip to Capri: Take a boat ride from Positano to the alluring island of Capri and learn how to create traditional dishes utilizing fresh local ingredients like handmade pasta, limoncello, and delectable seafood. Discover the renowned Blue Grotto, meander through Anacapri's quaint neighborhoods, and indulge in some upscale dining and shopping.

- Shopping for ceramics: Positano is renowned for its brilliant ceramics, and finding these colorful objects is a joy. To find one-of-a-kind and handcrafted ceramics, from tiles and plates to decorative pieces, visit nearby workshops and boutiques.
- Vallone dei Mulini: Pay a visit to Vallone dei Mulini to learn about Positano's secret history (Valley of the Mills). A interesting remnant of the town's industrial past, this abandoned flour mill is tucked away between cliffs and vegetation.
- Le Sirenuse Hotel: A visit to Le Sirenuse is a delight even if you aren't staying at this renowned luxury hotel. Take in the expansive views of the seaside while sipping on a beverage at La Sponda, the hotel's terrace bar.
- Kayaking and Boat Tours: Take a kayak rental or a boat excursion to see the Amalfi Coast from a different angle. Discover isolated beaches, grottos, and hidden coves while exploring the coastline from the boat.

3. Ravello

Ravello, a lovely and scenic village on Italy's stunning Amalfi Coast, is well-known for its breathtaking views, extensive history, and rich cultural legacy. There are many attractions and things to do in Ravello for tourists, including some undiscovered treasures. Let's explore Ravello's tourist hotspots and undiscovered wonders.

- Villa Rufolo: Villa Rufolo is a must-see sight in Ravello. This historic mansion is well-known for its stunning grounds, medieval architecture, and sweeping ocean views. Enjoy a leisurely stroll around the colorful gardens while being mesmerized by the breathtaking views.
- Villa Cimbrone: A stunning piece of architecture with lovely grounds and vistas is Villa Cimbrone. A standout feature of the property is the "Terrace of Infinity," which offers a stunning view of the Amalfi Coast. This undiscovered treasure is a tranquil haven away from the masses.

- Discover the Duomo di Ravello, a magnificent cathedral built in the 11th century, in the city of Ravello. Enjoy the cathedral's rich frescoes and stunning mosaics. The bronze doors, a masterwork of medieval art, are not to be missed.
- Ravello Festival: If you travel to the area in the summer, don't miss the Ravello Festival. This well-known music event presents a number of concerts that feature both classical and modern music. The festival takes place at numerous historic locations, giving your visit a special cultural touch.
- Learn about the history of papermaking in Ravello at the Paper Mill Museum (Museo della Carta). Learn about the conventional methods for making handmade paper. You may see the procedure in action and even make your own paper as a keepsake.
- The Valle delle Ferriere is a secret treasure for those who love the outdoors. A quiet paradise with waterfalls, this lush nature reserve is home to a wide variety of plants and animals. Hike through the valley's picturesque areas while keeping a look out for endangered species like the Woodwardia radicans fern.
- Visit the Auditorium Oscar Niemeyer, a cutting-edge cultural center perched on a hill, to learn more about contemporary architecture. Various creative performances and exhibitions are held in this distinctive building. From its patio, take in the expansive views of the surrounding scenery.
- Visit Torre dello Ziro for an excursion that is off the beaten path. The Amalfi Coast and Ravello are both visible from this historic tower's vantage point. Although the ascent to the tower is a little difficult, the serene environment and stunning views are the payoff.

- Ceramic Studios: Ravello is renowned for its fine ceramic work. Visit nearby ceramics studios to see how lovely hand-painted ceramics are made. Even better, you can take part in a class to master the skills and make your own special artwork.
- Take a leisurely stroll along the cliffside path that connects Ravello to other settlements like Atrani and Amalfi on the Ravello Cliffside Walk. Along the trip, savor the crisp sea breeze, expansive views, and beautiful coastal landscapes.

4. Praiano

On Italy's breathtaking Amalfi Coast is the quaint village of Praiano. Praiano has a distinctive appeal of its own and offers a variety of tourist attractions and activities, but perhaps not having the same level of fame as its nearby towns Positano and Amalfi. The village also has a number of undiscovered beauties worth discovering. Let's explore what makes Praiano such a terrific tourist destination.

- Gavitella Beach: Praiano is known for its stunning beaches, and Gavitella Beach is a little-known gem that shouldn't be missed. Compared to other of the busier beaches in the area, it provides breath-taking views, pristine waters, and a more relaxing ambiance.
- Path of the Gods: The Path of the Gods (Sentiero degli Dei) is a must-do activity for hikers and environment lovers. This historic trail passes through luxuriant Mediterranean flora and provides breathtaking panoramic views of the Amalfi Coast. The hike along the trail, which begins close to Praiano and ends in Positano, is a memorable experience.

- Church of San Gennaro: The Church of San Gennaro is a well-known landmark in Praiano and is significant in terms of both history and architecture. This gorgeous chapel has amazing frescoes and a bright dome. Inside, you can gaze upon holy objects and take in the tranquil setting.
- Discover the charming fishing community of Marina di Praia, which is tucked away in a tiny cove. You can enjoy a lunch at one of the waterfront eateries while taking a leisurely stroll along the harbor and seeing the vibrant vessels. There is a little beach area in the village where you may unwind and enjoy the sunshine.
- Fiordo di Furore: The charming Fiordo di Furore is only a short drive from Praiano. A deep valley that resembles a fjord and leads to a little beach is this hidden gem. Awe-inspiring scenery is created by the cliffs' dramatic features and the water's clearness. Swim in the clear waters or just take in the natural splendor of this remote location.
- Cooking classes: Praiano is famed for its delectable cuisine, and taking a cooking class is one of the greatest ways to get to know the community. Discover the secrets of Italian cooking while learning how to make classic dishes using local, fresh ingredients. This cooking experience is tasty and instructive.
- Boat Tours: Departing from Praiano, take a boat tour to see the Amalfi Coast from a different angle. For a guided trip or to find out about secret caverns, remote beaches, and towering cliffs, you can rent a boat. Observing the shoreline from the boat is a breathtaking and unique experience.
- La Praia is another well-liked tourist destination in Praiano. It is renowned for its crystal-clear waters and

breathtaking views of the coastline. Additionally, La Praia offers a variety of beach clubs and eateries where you may unwind and savor delectable seafood meals.

- Ceramic Workshops: Praiano is no exception to the Amalfi Coast's reputation for its traditional ceramic workmanship. Visit a nearby ceramics studio to see local artisans create elaborate designs and to buy one-of-a-kind handcrafted pottery as a gift.
- Last but not least, don't miss the chance to see the magnificent sunsets at Praia Beach. As the sun dips below the horizon, the sky transforms into a canvas of vibrant colors, casting a magical glow over the coastline. It's a tranquil and passionate encounter that perfectly encapsulates Praiano.

5. Valle delle Ferriere

For those looking for peace and beauty in nature, visiting Valle delle Ferriere on the Amalfi Coast is a delightful experience. This undiscovered gem is tucked away in the mountains behind the busy town of Amalfi and offers a tranquil retreat from the masses as well as an opportunity to fully see the breathtaking scenery of the area. The following list of tourist attractions and things to do in Valle delle Ferriere includes some undiscovered gems:

- Trails for Hiking: The Valle delle Ferriere region is well known for its attractive hiking routes that meander through luxuriant forests, charming waterfalls, and historic ruins. The Sentiero degli Dei (Path of the Gods), which provides stunning views of the coastline, is the most well-known trail. The Valle delle Ferriere Nature Reserve, which leads you through a protected region with a variety of flora and fauna, is one of the routes you can also explore.

- Waterfalls: The Cascata di Ferriere, a stunning waterfall that cascades down a rocky cliff, is one of the primary attractions of Valle delle Ferriere. Photographers and nature enthusiasts looking to capture the tranquility of the surrounds will find it to be the ideal location.
- Flora and Fauna: As a result of its microclimate and designation as a protected nature reserve, the valley is home to a wide range of plant and animal species. During your trek, you'll see unique ferns, orchids, and other Mediterranean plants. Be on the lookout for unusual types of birds, butterflies, and even the elusive otter, which occasionally inhabits the region.
- The relics of ancient paper mills, which previously played a significant role in the local economy, can be found as you explore the valley. You can discover more about the conventional paper-making method and its historical significance at these mills, which used to create the renowned Amalfi paper.
- You'll pass through charming hamlets and villages that are tucked into the mountainside as you travel. You can get a taste of everyday life in these communities and experience Amalfi Coast hospitality and culture for yourself.
- Swimming in the Emerald Pools: Throughout the valley, there are a number of natural pools created by the Canneto River's pristine waters. Especially in the summer months, these emerald-green pools offer a refreshing opportunity for a dip.
- Opportunities for Photography: Valle delle Ferriere is a photographer's dream. The breathtaking scenery,

waterfalls, and variety of species present countless opportunity for creating unforgettable images. There are many interesting subjects to choose from, such as expansive views of the shoreline and up-close photos of tiny wildflowers.

- Calm & Relaxation: The opportunity to get away from the throng and see nature firsthand is one of the real delights of touring Valle delle Ferriere. The tranquil setting of the valley, along with the soothing sound of the stream running and the rustling of the leaves, makes for a tranquil setting where you may unwind, think, and reenergize.

Keep in mind that Valle delle Ferriere is a protected region, so you should respect the surroundings and follow any rules that may be in place. Before starting any hiking trails, it's also a good idea to check the weather, pack water and snacks, and wear comfortable shoes.

6. Conca dei Marini

For each tourist, discovering Conca dei Marini on the Amalfi Coast is a lovely experience. This quaint Italian village, which is nestled between Amalfi and Positano, offers a combination of breathtaking natural beauty, cultural landmarks, and undiscovered jewels, making it a must-visit location. Here are some of Conca dei Marini's tourist attractions, including some of its best-kept secrets:

- The natural sea cave known as Grotta dello Smeraldo is a real jewel of Conca dei Marini. The Grotta dello Smeraldo is a captivating location to explore with its emerald-green waters and stunning stalactite formations. Inside the cave, visitors can take a boat excursion to experience its captivating splendor.

- Sacred Heart Monastery: The Santa Rosa Monastery, perched high atop a rock above the settlement, provides stunning views of the Amalfi Coast. The monastery's stunning architecture and serene atmosphere make it a welcome getaway. Don't pass up the opportunity to stroll through the lovely gardens and take in the expansive views.

- Located near the seaside, the Torre Saracena is a historic watchtower that provides sweeping views of the Mediterranean. The tower, which was constructed in the 16th century to stave off pirate invasions, today serves as a well-liked vantage point. For stunning views of the coastline and the glistening sea, climb to the top.

- Conca dei Marini is home to some stunning beaches. Fornillo Beach is a quiet pebble beach with crystal-clear waves and a serene atmosphere that may be found below the Santa Rosa Monastery. Another gorgeous beach, Marina di Conca, is renowned for its unspoiled beauty and tranquil environment.

- The Amalfi Coast is known for its beautiful hiking routes, and Conca dei Marini provides a number of possibilities for nature lovers. Famous trail The Path of the Gods (Sentiero degli Dei) offers breath-taking vistas of the shoreline. The Valle delle Ferriere, a lovely valley with waterfalls and luscious foliage, is another place you may go exploring.

- Local Cuisine: There are many top-notch restaurants in Conca dei Marini where you may enjoy authentic Italian cuisine. Don't pass up the chance to sample regional favorites including fresh fish, homemade pasta, and well-known desserts with lemon flavors like limoncello.

- Although less well-known than the neighbouring Fiordo di Furore, Conca dei Marini offers a lovely fjord of its own. It is a hidden gem that provides a tranquil haven with a little beach for swimming and tanning. It's a fantastic location for anybody looking for peace and quiet away from the bustle.

7. Fiordo di Crapolla

An undiscovered gem can be found in Italy's Amalfi Coast town of Fiordo di Crapolla. Visitors looking for a quieter and more private resort will find this magnificent inlet offers a distinctive and off-the-beaten-path experience. Following are some tourist attractions and things to do in Fiordo di Crapolla:

- Lovely Hike: Travel from Sant'Agata sui Due Golfi to Fiordo di Crapolla on a scenic hike. The walk provides stunning views of the coastline, luxuriant Mediterranean flora, and charming cliffside communities.
- Beach at Fiordo di Crapolla: Enjoy a leisurely day on the pebble beach here. Swimmable, snorkel-friendly seas make for ideal sunbathing and water activities. Rugged cliffs encircle the beach, giving it a sense of remoteness and quiet.
- Boat Tours: From adjacent cities like Positano or Sorrento, take a boat tour to Fiordo di Crapolla. This

presents special photo opportunities and enables you to admire the beauty of the shoreline from the water.

- Historical Ruins: Visit the remains of a former Roman residence close to Fiordo di Crapolla. These historical artifacts offer a fascinating window into the past and shed light on the region's rich history.
- Seafood Dining: Enjoy delectable seafood meals at neighborhood eateries close to Fiordo di Crapolla. The cuisine of the Amalfi Coast is known for its delicacies made from freshly caught fish and seafood. Don't pass up the chance to enjoy classic tastes in a gorgeous coastal location.

Now, let's move on to the hidden gems in the vicinity of Fiordo di Crapolla:

- Vallone di Furore: Vallone di Furore is a magnificent fjord-like inlet with clear seas that is only a short distance from Fiordo di Crapolla. For lovers of diving and snorkeling, it provides a tranquil haven.
- Marina di Praia is a secret beach that is tucked up between two enormous rocks. It is the perfect place to relax and take in the captivating surroundings because of its natural beauty and quiet.
- Sentiero degli Dei (Path of the Gods): The Sentiero degli Dei is a must-hike for intrepid hikers. This historic walk offers breath-taking vistas of the sea, cliffs, and terraced vineyards as it winds along the Amalfi Coast. It's a wonderful way to become fully immersed in the area's natural beauty..

Day trips while in Naples and Amalfi coast

Beautiful locations in Italy like Naples and the Amalfi Coast provide a wealth of day trip options for tourists. Some of the best tourist attractions and day trips you may take in these areas are listed below:

1. Pompeii and Mount Vesuvius: Explore the historic city of Pompeii, which was covered in volcanic ash in 79 AD and is now a UNESCO World Heritage site. Then, climb Mount Vesuvius for breathtaking panoramas of the region.

2. Capri: Visit the charming island of Capri by boat. Explore the lovely hamlet of Anacapri and the Blue Grotto, a spectacular marine grotto with iridescent blue waters. The stunning Augustus Gardens shouldn't be missed.

3. Sorrento: Visit Sorrento, a quaint town renowned for its aromatic lemon gardens and stunning views of the coast. Try some limoncello, a traditional lemon liqueur, then stroll around the historic district before exploring the area's small streets.

4. Herculaneum: Just a short train ride from Naples, Herculaneum (Ercolano) is another ancient Roman city that was buried by the eruption of Mount Vesuvius. Despite frequently being eclipsed by Pompeii, it has a comparably remarkable archaeological site. Discover the well-preserved remains, which include beautiful mosaics and historic structures and offer a fascinating look into Roman life.

5. Cilento National Park: Visit the stunning Cilento National Park, a UNESCO World Heritage site, on a day excursion. Take advantage of the hiking paths, tour

Paestum's Greek archaeological remains, and unwind on exquisite beaches like Marina di Camerota.

Chapter 3:
Itineraries

Five Days Itinerary

Day 1: Arrival in Naples and City Exploration

- Start your day with a visit to Naples' historic center, a UNESCO World Heritage site. Stroll through the narrow streets, admire the stunning architecture, and soak in the vibrant atmosphere.
- Visit the famous Duomo di Napoli (Naples Cathedral) and explore the adjacent treasure-filled San Gennaro Chapel.
- Head to Piazza del Plebiscito, one of the city's main squares. Take in the grandeur of the Royal Palace and San Carlo Opera House.
- In the afternoon, explore the fascinating underground tunnels of Napoli Sotterranea, which offer a unique glimpse into the city's history.

- End the day with a delicious Neapolitan pizza dinner at one of the city's renowned pizzerias.

Day 2: Day Trip to Pompeii and Mount Vesuvius

- Take a day trip to the ancient city of Pompeii, a UNESCO World Heritage site. Explore the remarkably preserved ruins and learn about life in ancient Rome before the devastating eruption of Mount Vesuvius in 79 AD.
- After visiting Pompeii, head to Mount Vesuvius. Take a guided hike to the crater and enjoy panoramic views of the surrounding area.
- Return to Naples in the evening and have dinner at a local trattoria, trying some traditional Campanian dishes.

Day 3: Arriving in Amalfi Coast

- Arrive in Naples and transfer to your accommodation in one of the towns along the Amalfi Coast, such as Amalfi, Positano, or Ravello.
- Take some time to explore the charming streets of your chosen town, enjoying the beautiful architecture and coastal views.
- Visit the famous Amalfi Cathedral in Amalfi or stroll along the picturesque beach promenade in Positano.
- Enjoy a delicious dinner at a local restaurant, savoring the flavors of traditional Italian cuisine.

Day 4: Exploring Amalfi

- Begin your day with a visit to the Museo della Carta in Amalfi, where you can learn about the region's historic paper-making industry.
- Take a boat tour to the enchanting Emerald Grotto (Grotta dello Smeraldo), known for its mesmerizing emerald-green waters.
- Afterward, visit the charming village of Atrani, located just a short walk from Amalfi. Explore its narrow alleys and enjoy the local atmosphere.
- In the evening, relax on the beach or find a cozy seaside restaurant to enjoy a delightful seafood dinner.

Day 5: Discovering Positano

- Spend the day exploring the beautiful town of Positano. Start by wandering through its colorful streets lined with boutique shops and charming cafés.
- Visit the Church of Santa Maria Assunta, known for its striking tiled dome and beautiful interior.
- Take a leisurely walk along the Spiaggia Grande, Positano's main beach, and enjoy some time sunbathing or swimming in the crystal-clear waters.
- Indulge in a delicious lunch at one of the seaside restaurants overlooking the beach.
- In the afternoon, consider taking a boat trip to the nearby island of Li Galli or relax on one of the smaller beaches like Fornillo.
- Celebrate your accomplishment with a delicious dinner in one of the local restaurants, enjoying the flavors of the region one last time.

One week itinerary

Day 1: Arrival in Naples

- Once you arrive, take a taxi to your hotel in Naples from the airport.
- Explore the crowded atmosphere and winding streets of Naples' old district on a leisurely stroll.
- Discover the riches of Pompeii and Herculaneum at the Naples National Archaeological Museum, which has a sizable collection of Roman artifacts.
- Visit a nearby pizzeria for a fantastic Neapolitan pizza meal.

Day 2: Naples Sightseeing

- Visit the Royal Palace of Naples (Palazzo Reale), a regal palace with beautiful architecture and sumptuous interiors, to start the day.
- Investigate the fascinating system of historic tunnels and caverns known as Napoli Sotterranea.
- Witness the magnificent mosaics and frescoes of the Duomo di San Gennaro, the cathedral in Naples.
- Enjoy stunning views of the Bay of Naples as you stroll along the charming Via Caracciolo waterfront promenade.

Day 3: Capri Island Excursion

- A full-day excursion to the alluring island of Capri is to be taken.
- Travel to Capri by ferry from Naples and take your time discovering the island.
- Visit the fabled Blue Grotto (Grotta Azzurra), a marine cave with enchanted waters that are a stunning shade of blue.

- Explore the charming town of Anacapri, located on the higher part of the island, and take a chairlift up to Monte Solaro for panoramic views.
- Experience the stunning vistas of the Faraglioni rock formations while taking a leisurely stroll around the Gardens of Augustus.

Day 4: Pompeii and Vesuvius

- Visit the historic city of Pompeii, which was destroyed by Mount Vesuvius' eruption in 79 AD, on a day tour.
- Discover Pompeii's well-preserved ruins, which include the forum, amphitheater, and the well-known victim plaster casts.
- Visit Mount Vesuvius, the volcano that towers over the Bay of Naples and is still active, after that.
- Enjoy panoramic views of the surroundings by hiking to Vesuvius' crater.

Day 5: Sorrento and Positano

- Travel to the charming village of Sorrento from Naples.
- Explore the charming streets of Sorrento, known for its lemon groves, stunning views, and delicious limoncello liqueur.
- Enjoy some free time for leisurely pursuits and shopping.
- Continue to Positano, a picturesque village known for its colorful homes that cascade down the cliffs.
- The afternoon can be spent lazing on the beach or discovering the little shops and cafés lining the winding alleys.

Day 6: Ravello and Amalfi

- Visit the Amalfi Coast's stunning vistas from the hilltop village of Ravello.
- Discover the stunning gardens at Villa Rufolo, which served as the source of inspiration for Richard Wagner's works.
- Continue to Amalfi, which was formerly a significant maritime republic.
- Explore the magnificent Amalfi Cathedral (Duomo di Amalfi) and take a stroll around the town's quaint alleyways.

Day 7: Free Day in Naples

- Enjoy a day off to continue your independent exploration of Naples.
- Visit the medieval Castel dell'Ovo, which is situated on the lovely island of Megaride.
- Investigate Naples' thriving street markets, such the Pignasecca Market or the Mercato di Porta Nolana.
- Enjoy regional delicacies including sfogliatelle pastries and customary seafood meals.
- Enjoy one more meal in Naples that evening while thinking back on the wonderful sights and activities you've had this week.

Weekend itinerary in Amalfi coast

Day 1:

Morning: Start your day in Positano, one of the most picturesque towns on the coast. Explore its narrow, winding streets lined with colorful houses, and visit the beautiful beach. Don't forget to snap some photos of the famous Positano view from the overlook!

Afternoon: Take a boat or bus to Amalfi, the namesake town of the coast. Explore the historic center and visit the stunning Amalfi Cathedral. Enjoy a leisurely lunch at a local trattoria and savor some fresh seafood or traditional Italian dishes.

Evening: Head to Ravello, a charming hilltop town known for its gardens and panoramic views. Visit Villa Rufolo or Villa Cimbrone to enjoy the stunning vistas of the coastline. Catch a concert at the famous Ravello Festival during the summer months or simply enjoy a romantic dinner overlooking the sea.

Day 2:

Morning: Start your day early and head to the town of Sorrento. Explore the town's historic center, visit the beautiful Duomo, and stroll along the bustling shopping streets. Don't forget to try some local limoncello, a traditional lemon liqueur.

Afternoon: Take a boat tour to the island of Capri. Explore the island's charming towns, such as Capri and Anacapri, and visit the famous Blue Grotto if it's open. Enjoy the crystal-clear waters by taking a swim or renting a small boat for a private excursion.

Evening: Return to the mainland and enjoy a relaxing evening in Maiori or Minori, two coastal towns known for their sandy beaches and tranquil atmosphere. Take a leisurely walk along the promenade and have dinner at a local restaurant, enjoying the fresh seafood and regional specialties.

Chapter 4:
Best Restaurants and Cuisine

The cuisine in Naples and the Amalfi Coast is renowned for its rich flavors, fresh ingredients, and traditional recipes. Here are 15 must-try local dishes and where you can find them:

- Pizza Margherita: San Marzano tomatoes, mozzarella di bufala, fresh basil, and extra virgin olive oil are added to the traditional Neapolitan pizza. Visit Da Michele, one of Naples's oldest and most renowned pizzerias.
- Spaghetti alle Vongole: Fresh clams, garlic, parsley, and a sprinkling of chili flakes over spaghetti. Try it at Ristorante Donna Rosa in Positano or Trattoria Da Emilia in Naples.
- Mozzarella di Bufala: cheese from Buffalo that is delicious and creamy. It is available in many

neighborhood markets, or you can go to a buffalo farm, like Caseificio Barlotti in Paestum.

- Sfogliatella: a sweet custard or ricotta filling inside a crisp, stacked pastry. Naples' Pasticceria Attanasio is renowned for its mouthwatering sfogliatelle.
- Linguine allo Scoglio: Pasta linguine with a selection of fresh seafood, including clams, mussels, shrimp, and squid. Enjoy this dish at Nerano's Ristorante Lo Scoglio.
- Ragu Napoletano: a pasta-friendly beef sauce that has been slowly cooked. Visit Trattoria Nennella or Trattoria da Carmine in Naples to try this filling dish.
- Gelato: Enjoy some rich, handcrafted gelato. For some of the best gelato in the area, visit Gay-Odin in Naples or Pasticceria Pansa in Amalfi.
- Frittura di Paranza: fried seafood mixture including little fish, anchovy, squid, and shrimp. Visit Trattoria da Ciccio in Sorrento to try it.
- Babà: a sponge cake with rum filling that is frequently served with chantilly cream or a cream filling. For the best babà, go to Pasticceria Poppella in Naples.
- Caprese Salad: A simple but delicious salad made with ripe tomatoes, mozzarella di bufala, fresh basil, and drizzled with olive oil. Sample it at Ristorante da Teresa in Positano.
- Zuppa di Pesce: A hearty fish stew made with a variety of local seafood and served with crusty bread. Enjoy it at Ristorante Lo Scoglio in Marina del Cantone.
- Lemon Delights: Try different lemon-flavored foods including lemon sorbet, lemon pastries, and limoncello (lemon liqueur). Visit the Ristorante Santa Caterina in Amalfi or the Limoncello di Capri store in Capri.

- Cuoppo: a cone-shaped paper stuffed with fried street food, such as fried fish, arancini (rice balls), and croquettes. Look for food carts in Naples' streets, especially in the city's ancient district.
- Alici Marinate: Lemon, garlic, and parsley are served with freshly marinated anchovies. Visit Naples' Trattoria da Emilia to have this meal.
- Pastiera Napoletana: A traditional Easter cake made with ricotta cheese, wheat berries, citrus zest, and flavored with orange blossom water. Find it at Pasticceria Scaturchio in Naples.

Top restaurants

Here are ten top restaurants in Naples and the Amalfi Coast that are highly recommended for visitors, along with their locations and famous dishes:

1. Il Comandante (Naples) Il Comandante, which is housed on the 10th floor of the Romeo Hotel, has breathtaking views of Naples. Modern Mediterranean cuisine is the restaurant's area of expertise. One of their signature dishes is the "Aria di mare" (Sea Breeze), a seafood dish with scallops, shrimp, and sea urchins.
2. Don Alfonso 1890 Restaurant (Sant'Agata sui Due Golfi). A renowned Michelin-starred restaurant named Don Alfonso 1890 may be found in the hills of Sant'Agata sui Due Golfi with a view of the Gulf of Naples. On their menu, they emphasize regional foods and classic tastes. Try their pasta dish "Scialatielli allo Scoglio," which features a variety of shellfish.
3. La Sponda (Positano). La Sponda is a classy restaurant housed in the opulent Le Sirenuse Hotel and renowned for its romantic ambiance and expansive views of the

Amalfi Coast. Their signature dish is the savory seafood risotto known as "Risotto ai Frutti di Mare."

4. Riccio, Il (Capri) Il Riccio, a Michelin-starred eatery in Anacapri, blends a magnificent beach setting with top-notch food. The "Crudo Mediterraneo," a menu of raw fish and seafood, is their specialty.

5. Restaurant da Emilia (Naples) Naples' Trattoria. da Emilia serves genuine Neapolitan food and is a favorite among locals. The "Parmigiana di Melanzane," a baked eggplant dish covered with tomato sauce, mozzarella, and Parmesan cheese, is their most well-known meal.

6. Luigi Scoglio (Nerano). The beautiful fishing village of Nerano is home to the family-run eatery Lo Scoglio. The pasta dish "Spaghetti alla Nerano," which is cooked with zucchini, cheese, and fresh basil, is a must-try.

7. Santa Caterina's Restaurant (Amalfi). The Michelin-starred restaurant at the opulent Santa Caterina Hotel boasts stunning views of the Amalfi Coast. Try their signature dish, the delicate pasta stuffed with ricotta and lemon known as "Tortellini di Ricotta e Limone."

8. Adolfo Da (Positano). Da Adolfo is a beachside restaurant famed for its rustic charm and delicious seafood, and it is reachable by boat from Positano. The "Spaghetti alle Vongole" and their grilled fish come highly recommended.

9. Zi'Ntonio (Sorrento). Zi'Ntonio is a family-run trattoria providing classic Neapolitan cuisine in the center of Sorrento. Gnocchi alla Sorrentina, soft potato dumplings in a delicious tomato and mozzarella sauce, are a must-try.

10. From the Sky, the Sea, and the Earth (Massa Lubrense) Da Ciccio Cielo Mare e Terra, located in the charming

village of Marina della Lobra, serves a beautiful fusion of seafood and land-based meals. For a great sampling of the regional fare, order their "Totani e Patate," fried squid with potatoes.

These restaurants showcase the diverse and delectable culinary offerings of the region, ensuring a memorable dining experience for visitors.

Chapter 5:
Accommodations in Naples
And Amalfi Coast

When visiting Naples and the Amalfi Coast, you'll find a wide range of accommodation options, from luxurious hotels to charming boutique properties. Here are ten top hotels in the region, along with their locations and amenities:

- Grand Hotel Vesuvio (Naples): This elegant 5-star hotel, which is seafront-located, features opulent rooms, a rooftop restaurant with panoramic views, a fitness center, and a spa.
- Romeo Hotel (Naples): This five-star hotel is located in the heart of Naples and offers contemporary and fashionable rooms, a rooftop pool and bar, a fine dining restaurant, a spa center, and a private harbor.
- Bellevue Syrene (Sorrento): This five-star hotel with a view of the Bay of Naples offers opulent

accommodations, a private sun deck with easy access to the water, a Michelin-starred restaurant, and a spa.

- Hotel Santa Caterina (Amalfi): This five-star hotel is perched on the Amalfi Coast's cliffs and offers stunning views, tastefully furnished rooms, a private beach, an infinity pool, and a wellness area.
- Le Sirenuse (Positano): This five-star hotel is housed in a lovely villa and provides opulent accommodations, a terrace with breathtaking views, a Michelin-starred restaurant, a spa, and an oceanfront swimming pool.
- Palazzo Avino (Ravello): This five-star hotel is housed in a 12-century palace that has been rebuilt. It has luxurious accommodations, a Michelin-starred restaurant, a rooftop terrace with a pool, and a wellness center.
- NH Collection Grand Hotel Convento di Amalfi (Amalfi): This five-star hotel is housed in a former 13th-century monastery and offers chic accommodations, a cliffside infinity pool, a panoramic terrace, and a spa.
- Hotel Caruso (Ravello): This five-star hotel, perched high above the Amalfi Coast, features opulent accommodations, a breathtaking infinity pool, a Michelin-starred restaurant, a spa, and exquisitely planted grounds.
- Villa Franca (Positano): This five-star hotel is perched on a hillside and offers stylish accommodations, a rooftop pool, a Mediterranean restaurant, a spa, and a free shuttle to the beach.
- Hotel Excelsior Vittoria (Sorrento): This five-star hotel has magnificent suites, a private port, a seaside pool, a Michelin-starred restaurant, and a spa. It is housed in

a historic building that looks out over the Bay of Naples.

From breath-taking views and swimming pools to fine cuisine and spa centers, these hotels provide a variety of services. These hotels provide travelers with opulent lodging, whether they desire a convenient location in Naples or a peaceful cliffside refuge along the Amalfi Coast.

Chapter 6:
Cultural Activities in Naples
And Amalfi Coast.

Naples and the Amalfi Coast are renowned for their rich cultural heritage and vibrant traditions. Here are ten main cultural activities you can experience in this region:

- Investigate the ancient archaeological remains of Pompeii and Herculaneum, which were preserved following Mount Vesuvius' eruption in 79 AD. Experience the interesting history firsthand and be amazed by the impressively preserved remains.
- Taking pleasure in Neapolitan Pizza: Since Naples is the origin of pizza, you must try real Neapolitan pizza. Visit a classic pizza to enjoy the thin, crispy dough and mouthwatering toppings.
- Admiring Art in Naples: Visit the National Archaeological Museum, which houses a sizable

collection of Roman and Greek artifacts, or check out the current art shows at the Madre Museum to learn more about Naples' vibrant art culture.

- Taking in a Traditional Opera: The Teatro di San Carlo is one of the most recognized opera houses in the world, and opera has a long history in Naples. Visit a performance to experience the magnificence of this art.

- Walking through the Old Town: Naples' Old Town is a UNESCO World Heritage Site and features winding alleys, hopping markets, and gorgeous Baroque buildings. Take a leisurely stroll and take in the lively environment.

- Travel by boat to the picturesque island of Capri, which sits off the coast, to explore. Explore the quaint hamlet of Anacapri, take in the breathtaking vistas, and go to the renowned Blue Grotto.

- Beaches on the Amalfi Coast to Enjoy: The Amalfi Coast is well-known for its stunning coastline and lovely beaches. In one of the coastal villages like Positano or Amalfi, you may unwind on the golden sands, swim in the azure waters, and enjoy the sunshine.

- Trying Limoncello: The Amalfi Coast is well-known for producing the liquor made from lemons called Limoncello. After learning about the manufacturing process at a nearby lemon garden, treat yourself to a sampling to appreciate the tart flavors.

- Festival celebrations take place all year long in Naples and around the Amalfi Coast. Participate in the fun at the Naples Pizza Festival, the Ravello Festival, which features concerts of classical music, or the Positano Procession of the Black Madonna.

- Explore the little village of Sorrento, which is renowned for its lemon-scented streets and stunning cliffside views. Visit the neighborhood artisan stores, stroll around the old district, and try the renowned limoncello cake.

These cultural activities offer a glimpse into the rich history, art, cuisine, and traditions of Naples and the enchanting Amalfi Coast.

Chapter 7:
Nightlife And Festivals In Naples and Amalfi Coast.

Naples and the Amalfi Coast are renowned for their vibrant nightlife, offering a mix of bustling city vibes and coastal charm. Here's a description of nightlife in various parts of Naples and the Amalfi Coast:

1. Naples: The nightlife in Naples is vibrant and diversified, offering something for everyone. The historic center is also known for its hip pubs, live music venues, and evocative cafes, especially in the neighborhoods of Piazza Bellini and Piazza San Domenico Maggiore. You can listen to a variety of music, including jazz and rock, and interact with both residents and visitors. Both Via Chiaia and Via Toledo are bustling avenues lined with a variety of taverns, clubs, and lounges.

2. Chiaia: Naples' posh Chiaia area offers a nightlife that is polished and upscale. You may find opulent bars, chic lounges, and rooftop terraces with expansive views of the bay along the picturesque waterfront promenade. Chiaia is renowned for its hip wine bars and cocktail lounges, where you can sample expertly made beverages and take in a more upscale ambience.

3. Posillipo: Posillipo is an upscale section in Naples.known for its expensive nightlife. High-end clubs and attractive venues can be found in the area, drawing a more affluent population. For guests looking for a chic nightlife scene, the mix of spectacular sea vistas, opulent settings, and top-notch entertainment delivers a remarkable experience.

4. Sorrento: Sorrento, which is on the Amalfi Coast, has a thriving and varied nightlife. Piazza Tasso, the town's bustling central plaza, is home to numerous pubs, cafes, and eateries. The lovely businesses that offer live music, karaoke nights, and DJ performances can be found all over the square's winding streets. A few clubs in Sorrento also cater to people looking to dance the night away.

5. Amalfi: Compared to Naples and Sorrento, the gorgeous coastal town of Amalfi boasts a more laid-back and mellow nightlife scene. Piazza Duomo, the town's lovely central plaza, becomes the center of action after dark. In these quaint bars and cafés, you may relax with a drink while taking in the charming ambiance. Despite not having many huge clubs, Amalfi is the ideal place for a leisurely evening stroll and a drink by the water.

6. Positano: Positano, another well-liked vacation spot on the Amalfi Coast, provides a charming and romantic

evening. Small taverns and homey eateries surround the town's winding streets, creating an intimate atmosphere. Some of the lovely experiences you can have in Positano include watching the sunset from a cliffside bar or taking in live music at a beachside cafe.

Festivals

The lively and colorful gatherings that make up the festivals of Naples and the Amalfi Coast region of Italy reflect the region's rich cultural heritage and customs. These celebrations provide tourists a one-of-a-kind and unforgettable experience while offering a glimpse into the way of life in the region. These prominent festivities will be taking place in Naples and around the Amalfi Coast.:

1. Feast of San Gennaro (September 19): This festival honors the patron saint of the city and is the most significant religious event in Naples. The highlight is the Miracle of San Gennaro, where the dried blood of the saint liquefies, believed to bring good fortune to the city. Processions, religious rituals, public performances, and fireworks are all part of the event.

2. Neapolitan Christmas Market (December): In December, Christmas markets and festive decorations animate Naples and the Amalfi Coast. These markets provide a wide selection of crafts, presents, and regional specialties, fostering a lively atmosphere. Visitors can take pleasure in Christmas mood, traditional food sampling, and shopping.

3. Amalfi Coast Music Festival (June to August): The summer months are dedicated to this yearly music festival, which presents operas, chamber music performances, and classical concerts. These musical

festivals draw music enthusiasts from all over the world to the scenic venues of the gorgeous seaside locations of Amalfi, Positano, and Ravello.

4. Pizza Village (June): This event honors the well-known Neapolitan food and is held in Naples, the birthplace of pizza. Pizzaiolos (pizza makers) from all over the world gather to showcase their skills, offering a wide variety of pizzas to taste. Live music, cultural events, and pizza-making competitions are all part of the event.

5. Ravello Festival (July to September): The Amalfi Coast's lovely hamlet of Ravello serves as the venue for this renowned music and arts festival. In stunning locations like Villa Rufolo and Villa Cimbrone, it includes a number of concerts, dance performances, and art displays. In a stunning environment, the festival features both national and international talent.

6. Feast of Sant'Antonio (June 13): The Amalfi Coast communities all participate in this celebration, which commemorates Saint Anthony of Padua. Processions, religious rituals, and street markets selling regional cuisine, confections, and handicrafts are all a part of the celebrations. People congregate to take in dancing performances, live music, and fireworks.

7. Festival of the Lemon (February to March): This vivacious celebration honors the famed citrus fruit of the area and is held in the town of Menton, close to the Amalfi Coast. With music and dancers in tow, elaborate floats decorated with lemons move through the streets. Visitors can partake of citrus-based delights, see the Lemon Queen crowned, and watch fireworks displays.

8. Feast of San Biagio (February 3This festival honors Saint Blaise, the patron saint of throat problems, and is held in the town of Sorrento. The saint's statue is

carried through the streets during a religious procession. The attendees are given a variety of regional treats, including the well-known "taralli" (ring-shaped biscuits).

9. Feast of Santa Rosalia (July 15-19): This event is held in Palermo, Sicily, but thanks to the substantial Sicilian immigrant population in the area, it also has an impact on Naples and the Amalfi Coast. Processions, music, street markets, and fireworks are all part of the festivities, which come to a dramatic conclusion with "The Triumph of Santa Rosalia."

10. Festival of the Madonna delle Grazie (September 8): This festival honors the Madonna and is held in Praiano, close to the Amalfi Coast (Virgin Mary). Traditional music and dancing are played as the Madonna statue is carried through the streets in a procession. The celebrations also feature religious rites, feasts, and artistic displays.

Chapter 8:
Souvenirs And Shopping in Naples & Amalfi Coast

Traditional crafts, upscale clothing, regional specialties, and one-of-a-kind souvenirs may all be found when shopping in Naples and the Amalfi Coast. The visitor shopping experience in these vivacious Italian cities is described as follows:

1. Naples: Naples is renowned for its vibrant markets and busy commercial areas. High-end stores and street vendors are just a few of the many alternatives the city has to offer. Via Toledo, a bustling boulevard studded with retailers, department stores, and chic clothing boutiques, is one of the most well-known shopping destinations. Fashionable apparel, footwear, accessories, and regional handicrafts are available here.

Markets like as Mercato di Porta Nolana and Mercato di Pignasecca are essential stops for people looking for regional produce and antiques. Fresh fruits, vegetables, seafood, meats, spices, and cheeses are available in abundance at these crowded markets. Local delicacies including limoncello, conventional ceramics, and handcrafted leather products are also available.

Naples is renowned for its artisanal products, including as cameos, coral jewelry, and nativity scenes (presepi). Visit the "Christmas Alley" on San Gregorio Armeno street to peruse stores selling exquisitely carved figurines and decorations.

2. Amalfi Coast: The Amalfi Coast is renowned for its scenic beauty and charming towns, where shopping is an integral part of the experience. Each town along the coast offers its unique shopping opportunities.

The village of Amalfi on the Amalfi Coast is famous for its thriving street markets, pottery stores, and handmade paper. Discover the shops on the Piazza del Duomo, where you can buy apparel, accessories, and pottery featuring renowned Amalfi Coast patterns.

Another charming village, Positano is well known for its fancy stores and boutiques. You can discover fine apparel, swimwear, sandals, and accessories here that are frequently manufactured from premium materials like linen and silk. Shopping fans will enjoy the inviting atmosphere that the bright exhibits adorning the winding streets have to offer.

With its galleries and stores showing regional artwork, ceramics, and complex mosaic works, Ravello is a sanctuary for art enthusiasts. The village is also well-known for its expertly constructed, handcrafted sandals. To find one-of-a-kind treasures, stroll the streets and peruse the shops.

A mix of upscale shopping and regional crafts may be found in the thriving town of Sorrento. Explore the fashion boutiques, jewelry stores, and gift shops on Corso Italia, the main shopping street. Don't forget to try the local specialty limoncello and look around stores selling goods with lemon flavoring.

Local delicacies like olive oil, spaghetti, limoncello, and Amalfi Coast wines may be found all along the Amalfi Coast. Don't pass up the chance to shop at neighborhood delis, wineries, and grocery stores to bring a piece of the area home with you.

Souvenirs

Naples and the Amalfi Coast in Italy offer a wide range of unique souvenirs that visitors can purchase to commemorate their trip. These souvenirs capture the rich culture, history, and beauty of the region. Here are some popular options:

- Limoncello: The traditional Amalfi Coast lemon liqueur is a well-liked travel memento. It is available in neighborhood booze stores and specialty stores in places like Sorrento and Positano.
- Ceramics: Ceramics that have been hand-painted are a traditional memento of the Amalfi Coast. In the stores and workshops in the town of Vietri sul Mare, which is well-known for its thriving ceramic production, you can find lovely items.
- Cameo jewelryThe magnificent cameo jewelry produced in Naples and throughout the Amalfi Coast is

well renowned. Look for delicate necklaces, earrings, and brooches featuring intricately carved shells. They are available in jewelry shops in Torre del Greco and Naples.

- Pizza Napoletana: By purchasing a pizza kit that includes the ingredients and directions for baking an authentic Neapolitan pizza, you can bring a piece of Naples home with you. In markets and specialty food stores all across Naples, you may get these kits.
- Limoncello ceramics: By choosing ceramic items with limoncello themes, you can combine two well-liked mementos. Look for plates, coasters, and decorative things with limoncello bottles and lemons on them. These are available in ceramics stores in cities like Positano and Sorrento.
- Espresso coffee: Espresso that has a lot of taste and is robust is famous in Naples. From one of Naples' storied coffeehouses, like Caffè Mexico or Caffè Gambrinus, take home a bag of locally roasted coffee beans or a box of ground coffee.
- Sfogliatella: This delicious pastry is a Neapolitan specialty. Visit historic pastry shops like Pintauro or Attanasio in Naples to try the freshly baked sfogliatelle and purchase a box to take home.
- Bottarga: Bottarga, a distinctive and savory condiment used in Mediterranean cooking, is made from cured fish roe. In Naples or other coastal cities like Amalfi, you can find this delicacy in specialist food stores or fish markets.
- Capodimonte porcelain: Capodimonte porcelain is a sought-after collector's item. Visit the Capodimonte Museum in Naples to see its impressive collection, and then head to local antique shops or specialized retailers

to find beautiful porcelain figurines and other decorative pieces.

- Anchovies: Salted anchovies are a well-liked regional ingredient and are a well-known component of Neapolitan cuisine. Purchase some premium anchovies from a neighborhood grocery shop or Naples' famed La Pescheria fish market.
- Taralli: These small, savory biscuits are a popular snack in Naples and the surrounding area. Look for them in local food stores or street markets, especially in Naples' historic center.
- Coral jewelry: The coral jewelry produced in the neighbouring village of Torre del Greco is well-known. In the town's boutiques and jewelry stores, you may purchase wonderful items made from red or pink coral.
- Marquetry boxes: Sorrento is renowned for its intricate marquetry work. Visit local souvenir shops to find beautifully crafted wooden boxes and other decorative items featuring delicate inlaid designs.
- Spaccanapoli postcards: Explore the vibrant streets of Naples and purchase postcards featuring the iconic Spaccanapoli, a long and narrow street that cuts through the historic center. Look for them in souvenir shops and kiosks around the city.
- Amalfi paper products: Amalfi is famous for its traditional paper production. Discover shops in Amalfi or Ravello that sell handmade paper products like notebooks, cards, and decorative items, often adorned with beautiful designs and patterns.

Chapter 9:
Tips For Traveling in Naples & Amalfi Coast.

These tips are a starting point, and there's so much more to discover in Naples and the Amalfi Coast.

- Plan your trip for the shoulder seasons: Compared to the busiest summer months, April to June and September to October provide pleasant weather and less crowding.
- Spend at least a few days touring Naples and the Amalfi Coast as the area has a lot to offer. Give yourself ample time.
- Consider taking public transit to get about. Examples include trains and buses. It's convenient and reasonably priced, albeit parking can be difficult to come by in some places.

- If you opt to rent a car, be warned that the coastal roads are congested and twisty. Be ready for small roadways. Driving should be done slowly and with caution.
- Try the local cuisine: Since pizza is synonymous with Naples, be sure to savor some real Neapolitan pizza. On the Amalfi Coast, try other local cuisines like seafood spaghetti and limoncello.
- Visit Pompeii and Herculaneum: Visit the well-preserved ruins of the ancient cities of Pompeii and Herculaneum for a look at Roman history.
- Take a boat excursion: Departing from Amalfi, Positano, or Sorrento, take a boat cruise to explore the breathtaking coastline. It provides stunning vistas and the chance to explore undiscovered beaches and coves.
- The Path of the Gods walk (Sentiero degli Dei) offers breathtaking views of the nearby mountains and the sea, so if you prefer trekking, you shouldn't miss it.
- Bring comfortable shoes; wearing them will make it easier to explore the towns and hiking trails in Naples and the Amalfi Coast, where the streets can be hilly and uneven.
- Pickpockets should be avoided, as they are in any big tourist attraction. Keep an eye on your possessions and stay away from carrying expensive stuff in busy places.
- Visit Capri Island: Go on a day excursion to the lovely island of Capri, which is renowned for its luxurious stores, breathtaking views, and the eponymous Blue Grotto.
- Explore the quaint coastal towns of Positano, Amalfi, and Ravello when you visit the Amalfi Coast. Each town offers magnificent views and its own distinct personality.

- Visit the neighborhood markets: Naples is home to a number of lively street markets, including Mercato di Porta Nolana and Mercato Pignasecca. Discover them to get a taste of the local culture and fresh produce.
- Respect local traditions: When visiting holy sites, Italians value manners and proper attire. Additionally, it's customary to say "buongiorno" (Italian for "good day") and "grazie" (thank you) after receiving services.
- The Amalfi Coast is famed for its breathtaking views and laid-back ambiance, so take a moment to unwind and take it all in. Spend some time relaxing, taking in the beauty all about you, and savoring the leisurely Italian way of life.

Conclusion

In conclusion, Naples and the Amalfi Coast provide an exceptional vacation experience rich in breathtaking scenery, extensive history, lively culture, and delectable cuisine. This travel guide has given readers a peek of the many sights and things to do in this stunning area of Italy.

Naples epitomizes Italian city life with its busy streets, historic ruins, and vibrant atmosphere. Visitors are taken on a voyage through time as they explore the archaeological wonders of Pompeii and Herculaneum and take in the splendor of the Royal Palace of Naples. The vibrant structures and bustling marketplaces that line the city's streets give visitors a real sense of the native way of life. Naples is a veritable refuge for food enthusiasts because of its world-famous pizza, which is a must-try during every visit.

Travelers are welcomed by breathtaking vistas of the azure sea, towering cliffs, and charming towns perched on the hillsides as they move along the Amalfi Coast. Positano, Amalfi, and Ravello, three picturesque villages, serve as a showcase for the splendor and allure of the area's architecture. Visitors can find hidden jewels, peruse small shops, and take in stunning views from cliffside vistas while meandering through the winding lanes. Additionally, visiting lesser-known villages like Vietri sul Mare and Praiano gives the excursion an additional sense of discovery and tranquillity.

For those who enjoy the great outdoors, the Amalfi Coast provides a wealth of activities. Adventurers are rewarded with amazing views and a closer connection to the area's stunning natural surroundings when they hike along the renowned Path of the Gods. Travelers can take boat excursions along the coast to discover secluded coves, grottoes, and immaculate beaches while submerging themselves in the Mediterranean's crystalline seas.

Naples and the Amalfi Coast offer an exceptional experience, whether you're looking for cultural immersion, historical exploration, culinary delights, or simply a relaxed vacation. It is the perfect location for all types of tourists because of its amazing architectural feats, breathtaking natural surroundings, and friendly people. Every traveler will find something to attract them in this region, from the energetic streets of Naples to the serene beauty of the coastline villages.

Pack your bags, live life to the fullest, and travel to Naples and the Amalfi Coast to experience their captivating landscapes and vibrant cultures. You will remember this experience for the rest of your life.

Made in the USA
Monee, IL
27 July 2023

40024280R00056